Lingo Dingo and the Norwegian Chef

Written by Mark Pallis
Illustrated by James Cottell

For my awesome sons - MP

For Leo and Juniper - JC

LINGO DINGO AND THE NORWEGIAN CHEF

Story edited by Natascha Biebow, Blue Elephant Storyshaping
First Printing, 2022
ISBN: 978-1-915337-29-0
NeuWestendPress.com

Lingo Dingo and the Norwegian Chef

Written by Mark Pallis
Illustrated by James Cottell

NEU WESTEND
— PRESS —

This is Lingo. She's a Dingo and she loves helping.

Anyone. Anytime. Anyhow.

Lingo often helps her stylish neighbour Gunther, who lives by himself next door. She does a few jobs and has a nice chat. It makes Gunter feel good and it makes Lingo feel good too.

One day, Lingo arranged a special birthday party for Gunther. She even ordered a cake from a famous Norwegian Chef.

There was a knock at the door, “It must be the cake!” said Lingo. But it was a monkey.

“Hallo. Mitt navn er Chef Nono. Jeg har et problem,” he said.

Oh no. I can’t speak Norwegian yet, thought Lingo. *Maybe ‘Hallo’ is like ‘Hello’.*

Hallo = Hello; **Mitt navn er** = My name is; **Jeg har et problem** = I have a problem

"Hallo," said Lingo. Chef Nono replied slowly, "Jeg beklager. Jeg kan ikke lage bursdagskaken."

"I don't understand," said Lingo. "But let me guess. You want..."

Jeg beklager = I am sorry; **bursdagskaken** = birthday cake
Jeg kan ikke lage bursdagskaken = I cannot make the birthday cake

En vogn = a trolley; **En sylteagurk** = a gherkin;
Ballonger = balloons; **Nei** = no

"Ovnen min er ødelagt," explained Chef.

"Kan jeg bruke ovnen din?"

Chef's oven must be broken thought Lingo. "I know! Let's bake the cake together," she said.

Ovnen min = my oven; **er ødelagt** = is broken;
Kan jeg bruke ovnen din? = can I use your oven?

Chef tapped his wrist. “Hva er klokka?
Ni? Ti?” he asked.

Lingo showed Chef her watch.

“Klokken elleve? La oss komme i gang! Rask.”
They only had one hour until the party.

Hva er klokka? = what time is it?; **Ni** = nine; **Ti** = ten;
Klokken elleve = eleven o’clock; **La oss komme i gang** = let’s go; **raskt** = quick

Chef Nono and Lingo whizzed around the kitchen:

Et forkle = an apron; **til deg** = for you; en visp = a whisk
En blandebolle = a mixing bowl

"Send meg smør, sukker, egg og mel," said Chef.

Lingo wasn't sure what those words meant, so she just grabbed fish, coffee and onions instead.

"Fisk, kaffe og løk. Motbydelig!" laughed Chef.

Send meg = pass me; **smør** = butter; **sukker** = sugar; **egg** = eggs; **og** = and; **mel** = flour; **fisk** = fish; **kaffe** = coffee; **løk** = onions; **Motbydelig** = disgusting

Chef plopped butter, sugar, eggs and flour into a bowl. “So that’s what ‘smør, sukker, egg og mel’ means!” laughed Lingo.

“Jeg blander, du blander, vi blander,” said Chef and together they began to mix the cake.

Jeg blander = I mix; **du blander** = you mix; **vi blander** = we mix

"Endelig, bakepulver. To skjeer," said Chef. Lingo guessed 'bakepulver' meant baking powder, but how much?

Before she could ask, Chef hurried away, saying, "Unnskyld meg, jeg må tisse."

Lingo laughed, "I can guess what 'tisse' means!"

Endelig = finally; **bakepulver** = baking powder; **To** = two; **skjeer** = spoonfulls; **Unnskyld meg** = excuse me; **jeg må tisse** = I need to do a wee wee

I wonder if this is too much? thought Lingo as she added ten spoonfulls of 'bakepulver' to the mix.

She carefully put everything into the oven and before long, a sweet cakey smell filled the kitchen.

proszek do pieczenia = baking powder

“Hva skjedde? Den er massiv!” said Chef.

Lingo realised she had added too much baking powder.

“Sorry,” she said sheepishly.

Hva skjedde? = what happened?; **Den er massiv** = it is massive

Katastrofe = disaster

"I know what will make you feel better," said Lingo, kindly. 'Eat this 'sylteagurk'!"

"Motbydelig. Jeg hater sylteagurk," said Chef.

They were running out of time.

sylteagurk = gherkins; **Motbydelig** = disgusting; **Jeg hater** = I hate

“I’ve got it! Gunther loves hats, so let’s turn the cakey mess into a hat cake! ” said Lingo.

First she shaped the cake, then she filled balloons with icing.

Next came the best part: POP! POP! POP!

It was a messy job but in the end, the cake looked fantastic.

“Rød, oransje, gul, grønn, blå. Fantastisk!” said Chef.

Rød = red; **oransje** = orange; **gul** = yellow; **grønn** = green; **blå** = blue; **Fantastisk** = fantastic

Døren = the door

Gunter was thrilled with his cake.

Chef's deep voice sang "Gratulerer med dagen..."

Gratulerer med dagen... = Congratulations on the day (Norwegian happy birthday song)

"Blås!" said Chef.

Gunther blew out all the candles in one puff and everyone tucked in.

Blås = blow

"Jeg spiser, du spiser, han spiser, hun spiser, de spiser," laughed Chef.

"Vi spiser!" added Lingo proudly.

jeg spiser = I eat; **du spiser** = you eat; **han spiser** = he eats; **hun spiser** = she eats; **de spiser** = they eat; **vi spiser** = we eat

The friends watched the sun as it set in the sky.

"Jeg er glad,
du er glad,
Vi er alle glade! cheered Chef.

jeg er glad = I am happy; **du er glad** = you are happy;
Vi er alle glade = we are all happy;

Baking a cake, helping a friend,
learning a new language... what a day!

But now it was time for bed. It was time to dream
about all the fun things that might happen tomorrow.

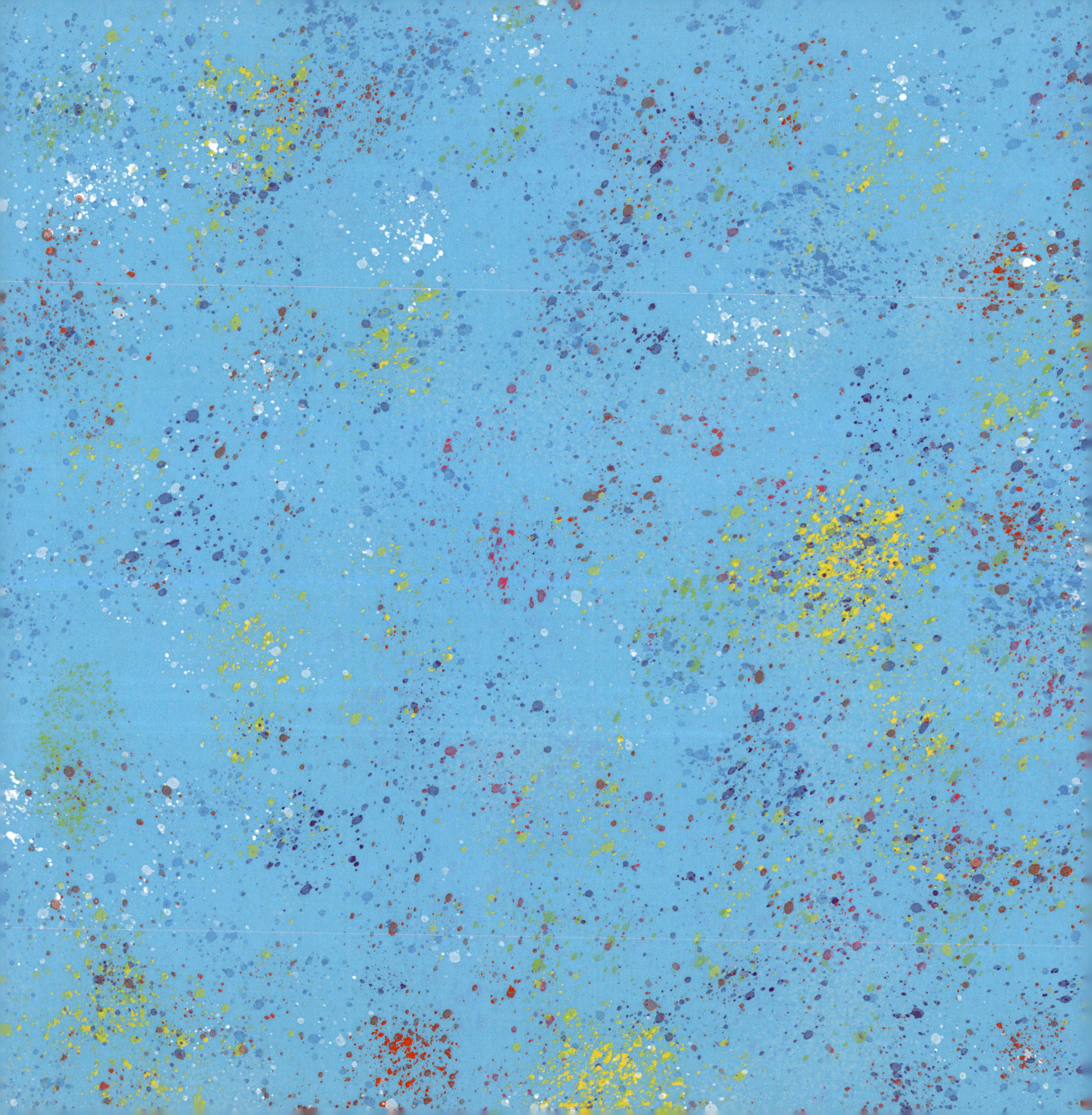

Learning to love languages

An additional language opens a child's mind, broadens their horizons and enriches their emotional life. Research has shown that the time between a child's birth and their sixth or seventh birthday is a "golden period" when they are most receptive to new languages. This is because they have an in-built ability to distinguish the sounds they hear and make sense of them. The Story-powered Language Learning Method taps into these natural abilities.

How the Story-powered language learning Method works

We create an emotionally engaging and funny story for children and adults to enjoy together, just like any other picture book. Studies show that social interaction, like enjoying a book together, is critical in language learning.

Through the story, we introduce a relatable character who speaks only in the new language. This helps build empathy and a positive attitude towards people who speak different languages. These are both important aspects in laying the foundations for lasting language acquisition in a child's life.

As the story progresses, the child naturally works with the characters to discover the meanings of a wide range of fun new words. Strategic use of humour ensures that this subconscious learning is rewarded with laughter; the child feels good and the first seeds of a lifelong love of languages are sown.

For more information and free learning resources visit www.neuwestendpress.com

You can learn more words and phrases with these hilarious, heartwarming stories from NEU WESTEND — PRESS —

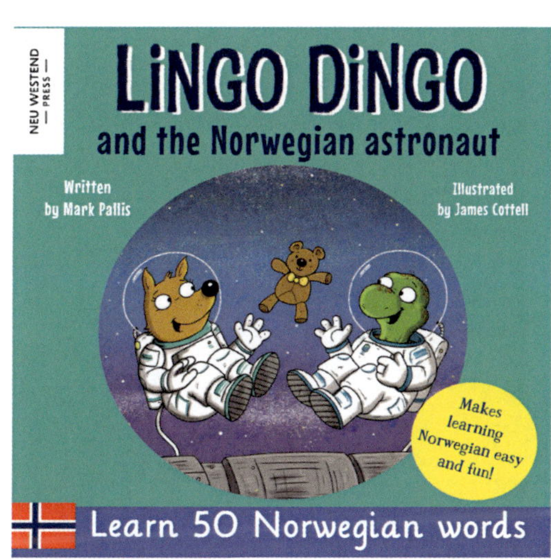

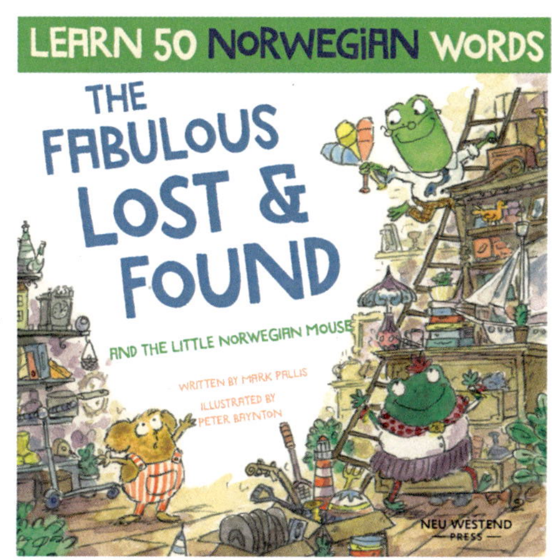

@MARK_PALLIS on twitter
www.neuwestendpress.com

To download your FREE certifcate, and more cool stuff, visit www.neuwestendpress.com

@jamescottell on INSTAGRAM
www.jamescottellstudios.com

"I want people to be so busy laughing, they don't realise they're learning!"

Mark Pallis

Crab and Whale is the bestselling story of how a little Crab helps a big Whale. It's carefully designed to help even the most energetic children find a moment of calm and focus. It also includes a special mindful breathing exercise and affirmation for children.
Also available in French, Italian, German & Spanish!
Featured as one of Mindful.org's
'Seven Mindful Children's books'

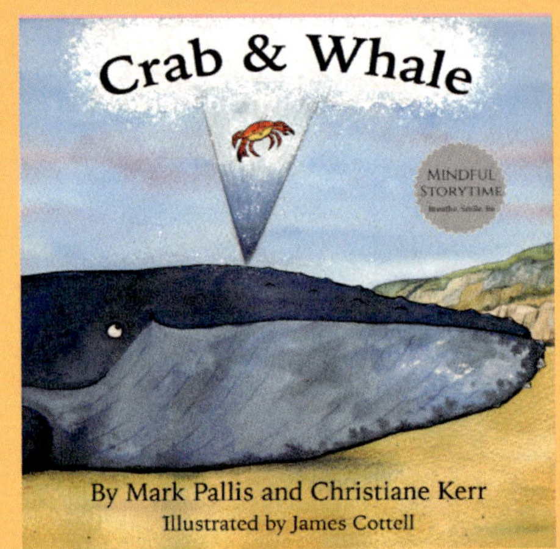

Do you call them hugs or cuddles?

In this funny, heartwarming story, you will laugh out loud as two loveable gibbons try to figure out if a hug is better than a cuddle and, in the process, learn how to get along.

A perfect story for anyone who loves a hug (or a cuddle!)

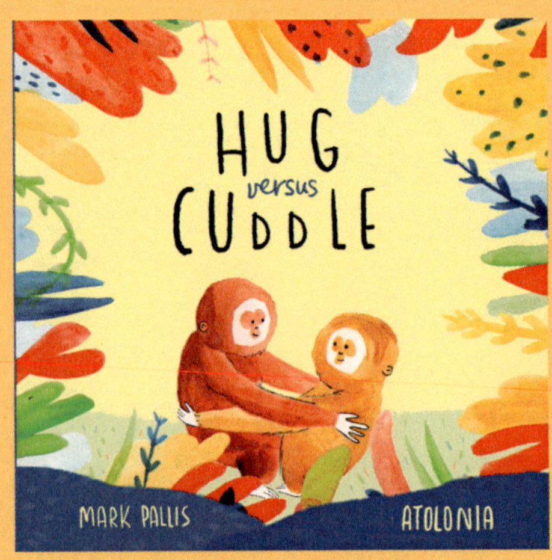

www.markpallis.com

Made in the USA
Las Vegas, NV
01 April 2025